Easy Olive Cookbook

An Olives Cookbook Filled with 50 Delicious Olive Recipes

By
BookSumo Press
All rights reserved

Published by
http://www.booksumo.com

ENJOY THE RECIPES?
KEEP ON COOKING WITH 6 MORE FREE COOKBOOKS!

Visit our website and simply enter your email address to join the club and receive your 6 cookbooks.

http://booksumo.com/magnet

https://www.instagram.com/booksumopress/

https://www.facebook.com/booksumo/

LEGAL NOTES

All Rights Reserved. No Part Of This Book May Be Reproduced Or Transmitted In Any Form Or By Any Means. Photocopying, Posting Online, And / Or Digital Copying Is Strictly Prohibited Unless Written Permission Is Granted By The Book's Publishing Company. Limited Use Of The Book's Text Is Permitted For Use In Reviews Written For The Public.

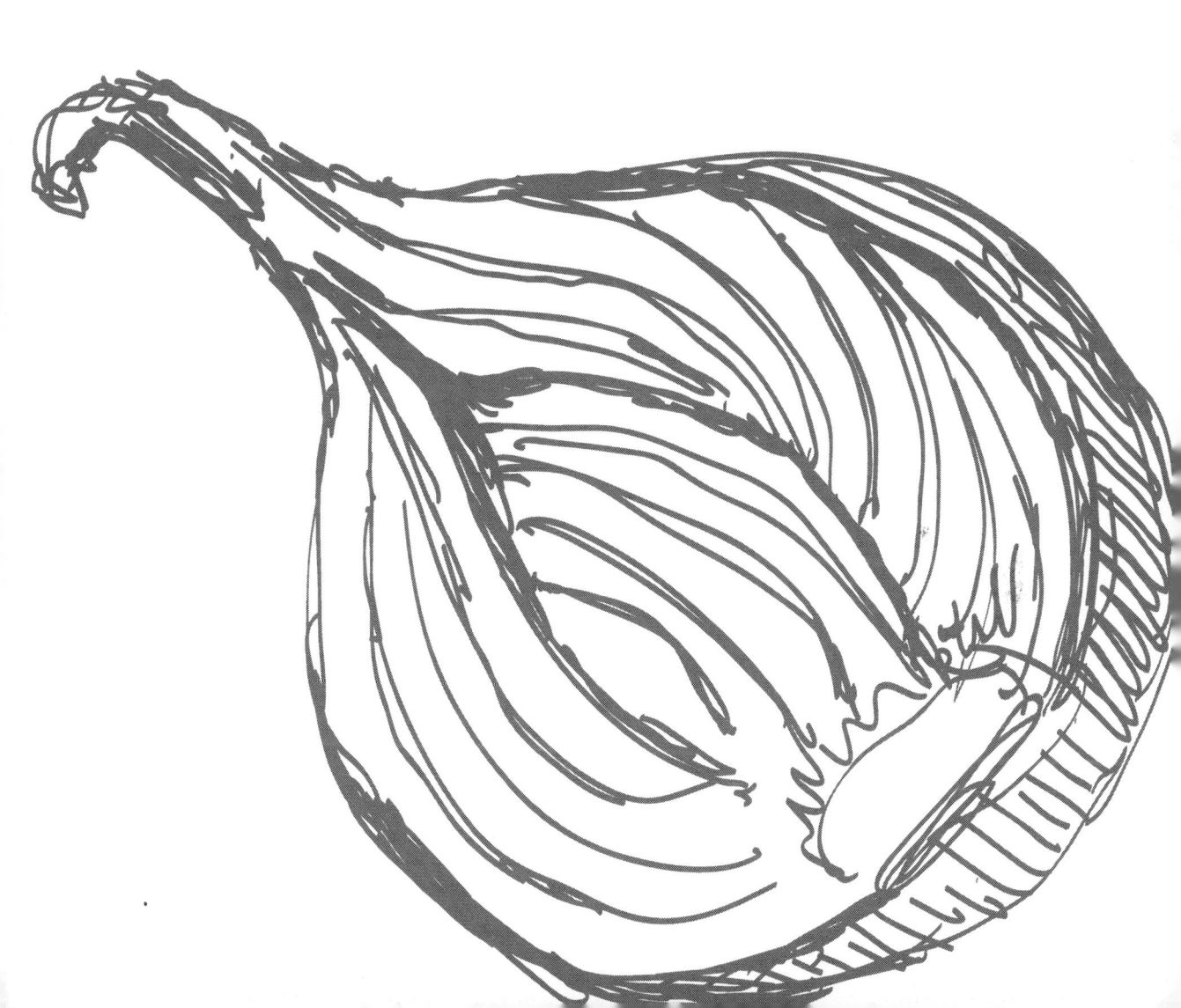

Table of Contents

Mediterranean Bread 7

Homemade Croutons 8

Mexican Festival Dip 9

Moroccan Dinner 10

Olivia's Favorite 12

Handmade Artisanal Olives 13

Aromatic Olives 14

Provence Tapenade 15

Easy Catering Stuffed Olives 16

Uptown Chicken Breast 17

2-Ingredient Olive Puff Pastry 18

Mediterranean Meatballs 19

Enhanced Cream Cheese Topping for Toast 20

Oven Focaccia 21

Louisiana Salad 22

Italian Antipasto Salad 23

Olive Balls 24

Complex Hummus 25

Roasted Rustic Olives 26

Olives for Dipping 27

Canadian Inspired Tuna 28

Mediterranean Salsa 29

Parmesan Pesto 30

Cooking Tuna Steaks 101 31

Skinny Girl Lunch 32

Alternative Chicken Breasts 33

Olive Toast Topping 34

Authentic Crostini 35

Garden Party Pizza 36

Lemony Greek Cake 38

Saturday Night French Pie 39

Mediterranean Burgers 40

Italian Mousse 41

Mediterranean Olive Hummus 42

Easy Fried Olives 43

Manhattan Party Appetizer 44

4-Ingredient Pot Roast Dump Dinner 45

Sophia's Dream 46

6-Ingredient Olives 47

Green Olive Lemon Chicken Breasts 48

Potluck Appetizer 49

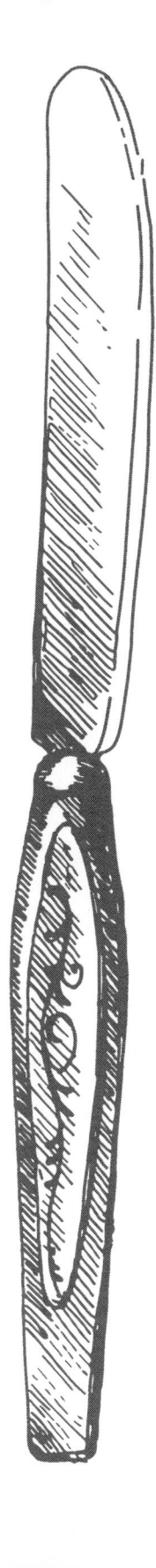

Greek Veggie Pizza 50

Vegetarian Orzo Pesto 51

Indian All-Ingredient Crepes 52

How to Make Deviled Eggs 54

Sun Dried Mediterranean Ziti 55

Kalamata Fettuccini 56

A Moroccan Dinner 57

French Italian Tilapia 58

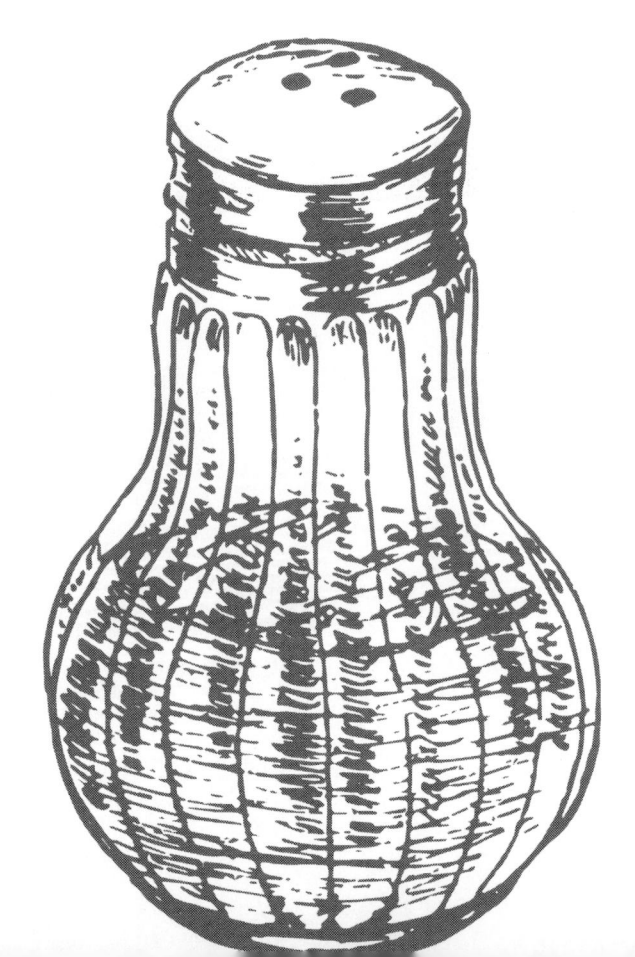

Mediterranean Bread

Prep Time: 20 mins
Total Time: 3 hrs 20 mins

Servings per Recipe: 24
Calories   186 kcal
Fat   3.6 g
Carbohydrates   32.3g
Protein   5.7 g
Cholesterol   0 mg
Sodium   384 mg

Ingredients

- 2 1/2 C. warm water (110 degrees F/45 degrees C)
- 2 tbsp active dry yeast
- 1 tsp molasses
- 2 tbsp olive oil
- 1 tbsp salt
- 7 1/2 C. bread flour
- 1 C. kalamata olives, pitted and chopped
- 2 tbsp chopped fresh rosemary
- 1 tbsp sesame seeds (optional)

Directions

1. In a bowl, add the water, yeast and molasses and stir to combine.
2. Keep aside till the mixture becomes creamy and foamy.
3. Add the olive oil and salt and mix.
4. Slowly, add the flour, about 1 C. at a time and mix till a stiff dough forms.
5. Stir in the olives and fresh herbs.
6. Place the dough onto a lightly floured surface and knead, adding enough flour and mix till a smooth and elastic dough forms.
7. Place the dough into a well oiled bowl and turn to coat the dough surface with oil.
8. Keep the dough for about 1 hour.
9. With your hands, punch down the dough.
10. Divide the dough into 2 equal sized pieces and form each piece into round loaves.
11. Place the loaves onto a greased baking sheet.
12. Coat the loaves with the cold water and sprinkle with the sesame seeds.
13. Keep aside for about 25-30 minutes.
14. Set your oven to 400 degrees F.
15. Cook in the oven for about 45 minutes.

HOMEMADE
Croutons

Prep Time: 10 mins
Total Time: 20 mins

Servings per Recipe: 4
Calories 191 kcal
Fat 6 g
Carbohydrates 28.7g
Protein 5.1 g
Cholesterol < 1 mg
Sodium < 365 mg

Ingredients

1 tbsp extra-virgin olive oil
1 tbsp tapenade (olive spread)
4 slices ciabatta bread, cut

Directions

1. Set your oven to 375 degrees F before doing anything else.
2. In a large bowl, mix together the olive oil and tapenade.
3. Add the bread cubes and stir to combine.
4. Place the bread cubes onto a baking sheet evenly.
5. Cook in the oven for about 8-10 minutes.
6. Remove from the oven and keep aside to cool completely.
7. Store in an airtight container.

Mexican Festival Dip

Prep Time: 20 mins
Total Time: 20 mins

Servings per Recipe: 28
Calories   42 kcal
Fat   3.2 g
Carbohydrates   1.9 g
Protein   < 1.8 g
Cholesterol   6 mg
Sodium   253 mg

Ingredients

1 (4 oz.) can chopped green chiles, drained
1 onion, chopped
1 (5 oz.) jar green olives, chopped (reserve brine)
1 (6 oz.) can chopped black olives
1 1/2 C. shredded Cheddar cheese
ground black pepper to taste
garlic salt to taste
2 fresh red tomatoes, chopped

Directions

1. Place a serving bowl into the freezer to chill.
2. In a mixing bowl, add all the ingredients and mix well.
3. Serve in the chilled bowl.

MOROCCAN
Dinner

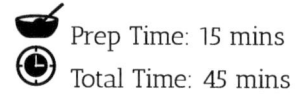

Prep Time: 15 mins
Total Time: 45 mins

Servings per Recipe: 4
Calories 645 kcal
Fat 37.2 g
Carbohydrates 7g
Protein 69.4 g
Cholesterol 208 mg
Sodium 1141 mg

Ingredients

4 boneless chicken breast halves with skin
salt and ground black pepper to taste
1 pinch cayenne pepper, or to taste
2 tsp herbes de Provence
2 tbsp olive oil
1/4 C. sliced shallots
1/2 C. pitted and sliced green olives
1/2 C. brine-cured pitted olives, such as Kalamata, halved lengthwise and brine reserved
1 C. chicken broth
1 lemon, zested and juiced
1/2 tsp cumin
2 tbsp chopped fresh flat-leaf parsley
2 tbsp cold butter, cut into four pieces

Directions

1. Season the skin-side of the chicken breast halves with the salt, black pepper and cayenne pepper.
2. Now, season the skinless side of the chicken breast halves with salt, black pepper, cayenne, and herbes de Provence.
3. In a large plate, place the the chicken breast halves, skin-side up and keep aside for about 10 minutes.
4. In a large skillet, heat the olive oil on high heat.
5. In the skillet, place the chicken breast halves, skin-side down.
6. Reduce the heat to medium-high and cook for about 5 minutes.
7. Carefully, flip the chicken and cook for about 2 minutes.
8. Transfer the chicken into a plate.
9. In the same skillet, cook the shallots on medium heat for about 2 minutes.
10. Stir in the olives and cook for about 30 seconds.
11. Add the chicken broth and bring to a boil, scraping the browned bits from the the bottom

of the pan with a wooden spoon.
12. Stir in the lemon juice, 2 tbsp of the the reserved olive brine, lemon zest and cumin.
13. Increase the heat to high and cook for about 2-3 minutes.
14. Reduce the heat to low and return chicken, skin-side up.
15. Cover the skillet and cook for about 5 minutes.
16. Transfer the chicken into a plate and with a piece of the foil, cover to keep warm.
17. Add the parsley and butter into sauce and cook till the butter melts, stirring continuously.
18. Place the sauce over chicken and serve.

OLIVIA'S Favorite

Prep Time: 20 mins
Total Time: 20 mins

Servings per Recipe: 50
Calories 60 kcal
Fat 6.1 g
Carbohydrates 0.8g
Protein < 1.1 g
Cholesterol 10 mg
Sodium 118 mg

Ingredients

2 (8 oz.) packages cream cheese, softened
1 (7 oz.) jar pimento-stuffed green olives
1/2 tsp seasoned salt
1 1/2 C. chopped pecans

Directions

1. In a bowl, add the cream cheese, seasoning salt, and 2 tbsp of juice from the olive jar and mix till well combined.
2. Refrigerate for about 30 minutes.
3. Place enough of the cream cheese mixture around each olive and cover completely.
4. Coat each olive ball with the chopped pecans and refrigerate till firm.
5. Cut each olive ball in half and arrange onto a serving platter, cut side up.

Handmade
Artisanal Olives

🥣 Prep Time: 1 hr
🕐 Total Time: 14 days 1 hr

Servings per Recipe: 32
Calories   135 kcal
Fat   14.6 g
Carbohydrates   2.5g
Protein   < 0.8 g
Cholesterol   0 mg
Sodium   1185 mg

Ingredients

4 lb. fresh ripe olives
10 C. water
4 tbsp kosher salt
2 lemons, sliced

1 C. olive oil
2 hot chile peppers

Directions

1. Rinse the olives and soak in a bowl of the cold water for overnight.
2. Drain the olives completely.
3. With a knife, make a small slit in each olive.
4. Fill the sterile pint jars with the olives.
5. cut the chile peppers into rings.
6. Place 1 chile peppers ring and 1 lemon slice into each jar.
7. In a bowl, dissolve the salt into water completely.
8. Place the salted water over the olives in the jar, leaving about 1/2-inch of space from the top.
9. Place the olive oil into the jars within 1/4-inch of the top.
10. Cover with the lids and seal tightly.
11. Refrigerate for 2 weeks before serving.

AROMATIC
Olives

🥣 Prep Time: 10 mins
🕐 Total Time: 2 d 10 mins

Servings per Recipe: 20
Calories	33 kcal
Fat	3.3 g
Carbohydrates	0.9g
Protein	< 0.3 g
Cholesterol	< 0 mg
Sodium	383 mg

Ingredients

1 (8 oz.) jar pitted green olives
1 (5 oz.) jar pitted kalamata olives, drained
2 bay leaves
1/4 tsp dried rosemary
1/2 tsp fennel seed
1/2 tsp dried thyme
6 tbsp distilled white vinegar

Directions

1. In a colander, add the olives and rinse under cool, running water.
2. Rinse the olive jars out with the water.
3. In a large bowl, mix together the bay leaves, rosemary, fennel, thyme and white vinegar.
4. Add the olives and toss to coat well.
5. Divide the mixture in the 2 jars. (make sure each jar gets one bay leaf.)
6. Fill any empty space with the water.
7. Seal the jars and shake well.
8. Refrigerate for at least 2 days.

Provence Tapenade

Prep Time: 15 mins
Total Time: 15 mins

Servings per Recipe: 8
Calories   81 kcal
Fat   7.9 g
Carbohydrates   2.5g
Protein   < 0.5 g
Cholesterol   < 0 mg
Sodium   359 mg

Ingredients

- 3 cloves garlic, peeled
- 1 C. pitted kalamata olives
- 2 tbsp capers
- 3 tbsp chopped fresh parsley
- 2 tbsp lemon juice
- 2 tbsp olive oil
- salt and pepper to taste

Directions

1. In a food processor, add the garlic cloves and pulse till minced.
2. Add the olives, capers, parsley, lemon juice, olive oil, salt and pepper and pulse till chopped finely.

EASY CATERING
Stuffed Olives

Prep Time: 10 mins
Total Time: 10 mins

Servings per Recipe: 50
Calories	148 kcal
Fat	14.4 g
Carbohydrates	3.4g
Protein	2.5 g
Cholesterol	31 mg
Sodium	455 mg

Ingredients

1 (6 oz.) can large, pitted black olives
4 oz. cream cheese

Directions

1. With a butter knife, fill each olive with the desired amount of cream cheese.
2. Serve immediately onto a decorative plate.

Uptown Chicken Breast

Prep Time: 15 mins
Total Time: 9 hrs 15 mins

Servings per Recipe: 6
Calories 402 kcal
Fat 22.4 g
Carbohydrates 16.5g
Protein 31.2 g
Cholesterol 97 mg
Sodium 308 mg

Ingredients

- 3 cloves garlic, minced
- 1/3 C. pitted prunes, halved
- 8 small green olives
- 2 tbsp capers, with liquid
- 2 tbsp olive oil
- 2 tbsp red wine vinegar
- 2 bay leaves
- 1 tbsp dried oregano
- salt and pepper to taste
- 1 (3 lb.) whole chicken, skin removed and cut into pieces
- 1/4 C. packed brown sugar
- 1/4 C. dry white wine
- 1 tbsp chopped fresh parsley, for garnish

Directions

1. In a bowl, mix together the garlic, prunes, olives, capers, olive oil, vinegar, bay leaves, oregano, salt and pepper.
2. Place the mixture in the bottom of a 10x15-inch baking dish evenly.
3. Add the chicken pieces and stir to coat.
4. Refrigerate, covered for overnight.
5. Set your oven to 350 degrees F.
6. Remove the baking dish from the refrigerator and sprinkle with the brown sugar evenly.
7. Place the white wine all around the chicken.
8. Cook in the oven for about 1 hour, spooning the juices over chicken occasionally.
9. Transfer the chicken mixture on a platter and top with the pan juices.
10. Serve with a garnishing of the fresh parsley.

2-INGREDIENT
Olive Puff Pastry

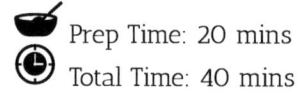

Prep Time: 20 mins
Total Time: 40 mins

Servings per Recipe: 12
Calories	230 kcal
Fat	16.2 g
Carbohydrates	18.3g
Protein	3 g
Cholesterol	0 mg
Sodium	265 mg

Ingredients

24 pimento-stuffed green olives
1 (17.25 oz.) package frozen puff pastry, thawed

Directions

1. Set your oven to 400 degrees F before doing anything else.
2. Cut the pastry into 6-inch long and 1/2-inch wide strips.
3. Wrap a pastry strip around each olive and arrange onto an ungreased baking sheet.
4. Cook in the oven for about 20 minutes.

Mediterranean
Meatballs

🥣 Prep Time: 10 mins
🕐 Total Time: 20 mins

Servings per Recipe: 8
Calories 185 kcal
Fat 13.7 g
Carbohydrates 1.5g
Protein < 13.8 g
Cholesterol 98 mg
Sodium 482 mg

Ingredients

1 lb. ground lamb
1/2 C. chopped fresh parsley
2 tbsp finely chopped onion
1/2 C. crumbled feta cheese
1/2 C. chopped green olives

2 eggs
1 tsp Italian seasoning

Directions

1. Set the broiler of your oven and arrange oven rack about 3-inch from the heating element.
2. In a large bowl, add the ground lamb, parsley, onion, feta cheese, green olives, eggs and Italian seasoning and mix till well combined.
3. Make 16 meatballs from the mixture.
4. Arrange the balls onto a baking sheet about 2-inch apart.
5. Cook under the broiler till browned from both sides.

ENHANCED Cream Cheese Topping for Toast

Prep Time: 10 mins
Total Time: 1 hr 10 mins

Servings per Recipe: 12
Calories   208 kcal
Fat   21.9 g
Carbohydrates   2.2g
Protein   < 2.5 g
Cholesterol   24 mg
Sodium   388 mg

Ingredients

8 oz. cream cheese, softened
1/2 C. mayonnaise
1 (5 oz.) jar sliced green olives, drained
1 C. coarsely chopped pecans

Directions

1. In a bowl, add the cream cheese, mayonnaise, olives and pecans and mix till well combined.
2. Transfer the mixture into a bowl and refrigerate for at least 1 hour before serving.

Oven Focaccia

Prep Time: 50 mins
Total Time: 1 hr 5 mins

Servings per Recipe: 8
Calories   287 kcal
Fat   11.8 g
Carbohydrates   37g
Protein   8.2 g
Cholesterol   4 mg
Sodium   448 mg

Ingredients

Focaccia Dough
- 1 C. warm water (100 to 110 degrees)
- 1 tsp white sugar
- 1 (.25 oz.) envelope rapid rise yeast
- 2 tbsp olive oil
- 1/4 C. minced fresh rosemary
- 2 3/4 C. bread flour or all-purpose flour
- 1 tsp salt
- 1/2 C. pitted black olives

Topping
- 3 tbsp olive oil
- 2 large roma (plum) tomatoes, sliced
- 2 tsp minced garlic
- 2 tbsp minced fresh rosemary
- Salt and pepper
- 1/2 C. grated Parmesan cheese

Directions

1. In a bowl, dissolve the sugar and yeast in water and keep aside for about 5 minutes.
2. Add 2 tbsp of the olive oil, 1/4 C. of the rosemary, flour and salt and mix till a dough forms.
3. Place the dough onto a lightly floured surface and knead till smooth and elastic.
4. In the last few minutes gently, knead in the black olives.
5. Transfer the dough into a lightly oiled bowl.
6. With a towel, cover the bowl and keep in a warm place for about 30 minutes.
7. Set your oven to 400 degrees F and grease a baking sheet.
8. transfer the dough into the prepared baking sheet and press to smooth.
9. Coat the dough with 1 tbsp of the olive oil.
10. In a bowl, add sliced tomatoes, garlic, remaining 2 tbsp of the olive oil, 2 tbsp of the minced rosemary, salt and pepper and toss to coat well.
11. Place the tomato slices over the dough in an even layer and sprinkle with the grated cheese. Cook in the oven for about 15-20 minutes.
12. Cut into the squares and serve immediately.

LOUISIANA
Salad

Prep Time: 10 mins
Total Time: 10 mins

Servings per Recipe: 8
Calories 193 kcal
Fat 19.3 g
Carbohydrates 6 g
Protein 1.5 g
Cholesterol 0 mg
Sodium 692 mg

Ingredients

1 (6 oz.) can black olives, drained
1 (5 oz.) jar pitted green olives, rinsed and drained
1 (6.5 oz.) jar marinated artichoke hearts, undrained
1 small red onion, chopped
1/4 C. red wine vinegar
1/2 C. olive oil
1 tsp dried minced garlic
1/2 tsp celery seed
1 tsp dried oregano
1 tsp dried basil
3/4 tsp black pepper

Directions

1. In a food processor, add all the ingredients and pulse till chopped finely.
2. This salad will be great for sandwiches or as as a dip for the crackers.

Italian Antipasto Salad

Prep Time: 30 mins
Total Time: 3 hrs 30 mins

Servings per Recipe: 8
Calories   428 kcal
Fat   32.8 g
Carbohydrates   16.4g
Protein   17.7 g
Cholesterol   51 mg
Sodium   1358 mg

Ingredients

3 (6.5 oz.) jars marinated artichoke hearts, undrained
1 (12 oz.) jar roasted red bell peppers, drained and sliced
1 (15 oz.) can black olives, drained
1 lb. smoked provolone cheese, diced
1/3 C. olive oil
1/2 C. balsamic vinegar
1/2 tsp dried oregano

1 clove garlic, finely chopped
1 pinch salt and pepper to taste
8 fresh basil leaves, cut into thin strips

Directions

1. In a 1 1/2 quart container with a tight sealing lid, place the jars of artichoke hearts with their liquid, bell peppers, black olives and provolone cheese.
2. In a bowl, add the olive oil, balsamic vinegar, oregano, garlic, salt and pepper and beat till well combined.
3. Place the olive oil mixture over the ingredients in the container.
4. Seal the lid tightly and refrigerate for at least 3 hours, shaking gently after every 1 hour.
5. Remove from the refrigerator and keep aside to come to room temperature before serving.
6. Divide the mixture into serving plates and serve with a garnishing of the basil shreds.

OLIVE Balls

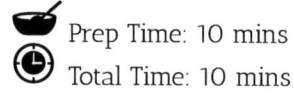

Prep Time: 10 mins
Total Time: 10 mins

Servings per Recipe: 10
Calories	165 kcal
Fat	16 g
Carbohydrates	1g
Protein	< 4.7 g
Cholesterol	44 mg
Sodium	447 mg

Ingredients

1 (8 oz.) package cream cheese, softened
3 tbsp butter, softened
1 C. crumbled bleu cheese

1 tbsp chopped fresh chives
1/2 C. chopped green olives

Directions

1. In a medium bowl, add the cream cheese, butter and blue cheese and mix till well combined.
2. Stir in the olives and chives.
3. Place the mixture onto a plastic wrap and roll into a ball.
4. Refrigerate for at least 30 minutes before serving.
5. Before serving, remove the plastic wrap and arrange onto a serving tray.
6. Serve with your favorite crackers.

Complex Hummus

Prep Time: 5 mins
Total Time: 5 mins

Servings per Recipe: 6
Calories	130 kcal
Fat	8.3 g
Carbohydrates	11.9 g
Protein	2.5 g
Cholesterol	0 mg
Sodium	424 mg

Ingredients

- 1 (15 oz.) can garbanzo beans, drained
- 1/3 C. pimento-stuffed Manzanilla olives
- 1/4 C. lemon juice
- 2 cloves garlic, minced
- 3 tbsp extra-virgin olive oil
- 2 tsp chopped fresh basil
- 1 1/2 tsp chopped fresh parsley
- 1/4 tsp salt, or to taste
- 1/8 tsp ground black pepper

Directions

1. In a food processor, add all the ingredients and pulse till smooth.

ROASTED
Rustic Olives

Prep Time: 25 mins
Total Time: 40 mins

Servings per Recipe: 12
Calories 75 kcal
Fat 7.5 g
Carbohydrates 1.4g
Protein < 0.7 g
Cholesterol 0 mg
Sodium 981 mg

Ingredients

3 1/2 C. whole mixed olives, drained
1/4 C. dry white wine
2 tbsp fresh orange juice
2 tbsp olive oil
2 cloves garlic, minced
2 sprigs fresh rosemary
2 tbsp fresh parsley, chopped
1 1/2 tbsp chopped fresh oregano
4 tsp grated orange zest
1/4 tsp crushed red pepper flakes

Directions

1. Set your oven to 375 degrees F before doing anything else.
2. In a 13x9-inch baking dish, mix together the olives, wine, orange juice, olive oil and garlic.
3. Press the rosemary sprigs in the olives mixture.
4. Cook in the oven for about 15 minutes, stirring once in the middle way.
5. Remove the rosemary sprigs.
6. Add the parsley, oregano, orange zest and red pepper flakes and stir to combine.
7. These baked olives can be served warm or cool as well.

Olives for Dipping

Prep Time: 5 mins
Total Time: 10 mins

Servings per Recipe: 16
Calories   127 kcal
Fat   14 g
Carbohydrates   0.2g
Protein   < 0.1 g
Cholesterol   < 0 mg
Sodium   < 1 mg

Ingredients

1 C. extra-virgin olive oil
2 cloves garlic, minced
1/4 tsp dried oregano
1 pinch salt
1 pinch dried rosemary
1 pinch dried basil
ground black pepper to taste

Directions

1. In a skillet, mix together all the ingredients on medium heat and cook for about 5 minutes.
2. Immediately, remove from the heat.

CANADIAN
Inspired Tuna

🥣 Prep Time: 10 mins
🕐 Total Time: 25 mins

Servings per Recipe: 4
Calories	649 kcal
Fat	30.1 g
Carbohydrates	49.3g
Protein	43.3 g
Cholesterol	102 mg
Sodium	1088 mg

Ingredients

2 tbsp butter
1/2 large sweet red onion, thinly sliced
1 tbsp maple syrup
2 (6 oz.) cans tuna, drained
2 tbsp creamy salad dressing (such as Miracle Whip(R))
salt and ground black pepper to taste
1 (12 oz.) loaf Italian olive bread
8 oz. shredded Cheddar cheese

Directions

1. In a small frying pan, melt the butter on medium heat and sauté the onion for about 3 minutes.
2. Reduce the heat to medium-low and stir in the maple syrup.
3. Cook for about 7-10 minutes.
4. Set the broiler of your oven and arrange oven rack about 8-inches from the heating element.
5. In a bowl, mix together the tuna, salad dressing, salt and pepper.
6. Cut the bread loaf in half horizontally.
7. Now, cut the both pieces in half lengthwise, making four equal pieces.
8. Place bread the bread pieces onto a baking sheet, crust-side down.
9. Place the tuna mixture, onion, and Cheddar cheese over the bread pieces evenly.
10. Cook under the broiler for about 5 minutes.

Mediterranean Salsa

Prep Time: 15 mins
Total Time: 15 mins

Servings per Recipe: 25
Calories   38 kcal
Fat   3.5 g
Carbohydrates   2g
Protein   < 0.4 g
Cholesterol   < 0 mg
Sodium   317 mg

Ingredients

1 1/2 (5 oz.) jars green olives (such as Italica(R))
1 (6 oz.) can pitted black olives
1 (4 oz.) can chopped green chilies
1 large white onion, cut into large chunks
2 tomatoes, cored
3 tbsp olive oil
1 1/2 tbsp red wine vinegar
4 cloves garlic, peeled
3 drops hot pepper sauce (such as Tabasco(R))

Directions

1. In a colander, drain the green and black olives and green chiles.
2. In a food processor, chop the white onion.
3. Add the green and black olives, green chiles, tomatoes, olive oil, red wine vinegar, garlic and hot sauce and pulse till chunky.

PARMESAN
Pesto

🍳 Prep Time: 10 mins
🕐 Total Time: 10 mins

Servings per Recipe: 8
Calories   123 kcal
Fat   12.5 g
Carbohydrates   2.4g
Protein   < 1.6 g
Cholesterol   1 mg
Sodium   < 179 mg

Ingredients

1 C. pitted olives
1 C. fresh parsley
1/3 C. walnuts
1/4 C. olive oil

2 tbsp grated Parmesan cheese
1 clove garlic

Directions

1. In a food processor, add all the ingredients and pulse till well combined.

Cooking Tuna Steaks 101

Prep Time: 10 mins
Total Time: 1 d 1 h 20 m

Servings per Recipe: 2
Calories 608 kcal
Fat 36 g
Carbohydrates 1.3g
Protein < 66.5 g
Cholesterol 109 mg
Sodium 271 mg

Ingredients

- 2 (10 oz.) thick-cut ahi tuna steaks
- 2 cloves garlic, bruised
- 6 sprigs fresh thyme
- 1 pinch red pepper flakes
- 2 C. olive oil
- sea salt to taste

Directions

1. Keep the tuna in room temperature for about 10-15 minutes before using.
2. In a heavy skillet, heat about 1-inch of oil on medium heat and cook the garlic, thyme and red pepper flakes for about 5-10 minutes.
3. Gently, place the tuna in the skillet and reduce the heat to low.
4. Cook the steaks for about 5-7 minutes, spooning the oil over the steaks continuously.
5. Remove from the heat and transfer the tuna steaks onto to a baking dish.
6. Place the hot oil and herbs over the the tuna steaks evenly.
7. Keep in the room temperature to cool completely.
8. With a plastic wrap, cover the baking dish tightly and refrigerate for about 24 hours.
9. Remove the tuna steaks from the oil and sprinkle with the sea salt.

SKINNY GIRL
Lunch

Prep Time: 5 mins
Total Time: 15 mins

Servings per Recipe: 2
Calories 169 kcal
Fat 13.9 g
Carbohydrates 10.7g
Protein 2.7 g
Cholesterol 0 mg
Sodium 291 mg

Ingredients

1 tbsp olive oil
1 clove garlic, minced
2 C. cherry tomatoes
2 tsp balsamic vinegar

1/4 C. pitted kalamata olives
1 tbsp pine nuts (optional)
ground black pepper to taste

Directions

1. In a large skillet, heat the olive oil on medium-high heat and sauté the garlic, tomatoes for about 7 minutes.
2. Stir in the olives, pine nuts and pepper and cook for about 3 minutes.

Alternative Chicken Breasts

Prep Time: 15 mins
Total Time: 1 hr 20 mins

Servings per Recipe: 4
Calories   223 kcal
Fat   10.9 g
Carbohydrates   11.7 g
Protein   19.3 g
Cholesterol   46 mg
Sodium   1557 mg

Ingredients

- 2 tsp vegetable oil
- 3 small boneless skinless chicken breasts, cut into chunks
- 3 slices turkey bacon, cut into 1/2-inch wide strips
- 1 C. water
- 2 (10 oz.) cans tomato sauce
- 3/4 C. green olives with pimientos
- 5 cloves garlic
- 2 tbsp vermouth
- 2 tbsp lemon juice
- 1/2 tbsp red pepper flakes

Directions

1. In a Dutch oven, heat the vegetable oil on medium-high heat and cook the chicken and bacon for about 5-10 minutes.
2. Drain the oil, leaving chicken and bacon in the Dutch oven.
3. Add the water and bring to a boil, scraping the browned bits from the bottom with a wooden spoon.
4. Stir in the tomato sauce, green olives, garlic, vermouth, lemon juice and red pepper flakes.
5. Reduce the heat to medium and and simmer for about 1 hour, stirring occasionally.

OLIVE TOAST
Topping

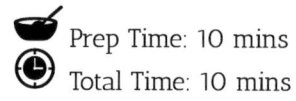

Prep Time: 10 mins
Total Time: 10 mins

Servings per Recipe: 40
Calories	62 kcal
Fat	6.3 g
Carbohydrates	1.4g
Protein	< 0.8 g
Cholesterol	1 mg
Sodium	< 124 mg

Ingredients

3 C. pitted black olives
1 1/2 C. chopped walnuts
1/2 C. mayonnaise
1 tbsp sour cream
1 tsp dried thyme
1/4 tsp ground black pepper

1/4 tsp salt
1/2 tsp garlic powder
1/4 tsp dried minced onion

Directions

1. In a food processor, add all the ingredients and pulse till well combined.
2. Transfer the mixture into a bowl and refrigerate to chill before serving.

Authentic Crostini

🥣 Prep Time: 20 mins
🕐 Total Time: 30 mins

Servings per Recipe: 6
Calories   55 kcal
Fat   4.8 g
Carbohydrates   0.5g
Protein   < 2.8 g
Cholesterol   76 mg
Sodium   86 mg

Ingredients

- 6 eggs
- 1 (3 oz.) package cream cheese, softened
- 1 tbsp lemon juice
- 1 tsp prepared Dijon-style mustard
- 1/4 tsp ground black pepper
- 2 tbsp sliced pimento-stuffed green olives
- 1 tbsp chopped fresh chives
- 1 tbsp olive oil
- paprika

Directions

1. In a pan, add the eggs and enough water to cover and bring to a boil.
2. Immediately, remove from the heat and keep aside, covered for about 10-12 minutes.
3. Remove from hot water and rinse under cold water to cool.
4. Peel the eggs and chop.
5. Set your oven to 375 degrees F and lightly, grease a large baking sheet.
6. In a bowl, add the cream cheese, lemon juice, prepared Dijon-style mustard and ground black pepper and mix till well combined.
7. Stir in the chopped eggs, olives and chives.
8. Cut each bread slice into 4 triangles.
9. Create a shallow hollow on the face of each slice triangle.
10. Coat the slices with the olive oil evenly.
11. Fill each hollowed slice with the olives mixture.
12. Place the slices onto the prepared baking sheet in a single layer.
13. Cook in the oven for about 10 minutes.
14. Serve with a sprinkling of the paprika

GARDEN PARTY
Pizza

🥣 Prep Time: 25 mins
🕐 Total Time: 30 mins

Servings per Recipe: 6
Calories   353 kcal
Fat   17.8 g
Carbohydrates   32.1g
Protein   16.8 g
Cholesterol   30 mg
Sodium   1150 mg

Ingredients

3 medium tomatoes
2 tbsp olive oil
1/2 tsp salt
1/4 tsp pepper
1 tbsp dried tarragon
5 cloves garlic, minced
1/3 C. drained canned cannellini beans
1/4 C. canned mushrooms, drained
1 tsp poultry seasoning
1 tsp garlic powder
2 1/2 C. shredded mozzarella cheese
1/2 C. sliced black olives
3 (10 inch) flour tortillas

Directions

1. Set your oven to 375 degrees F before doing anything else.
2. In a pan of boiling water, boil the tomatoes for about 5 minutes.
3. drain the tomatoes and transfer into a bowl of cold water.
4. Peel the tomatoes and cut in half.
5. Arrange the tomato halves onto a baking sheet, cut side up.
6. Drizzle with the olive oil and sprinkle with the salt, pepper and some tarragon.
7. (Reserve 1 tsp of tarragon for later.)
8. Cook in the oven for about 12 minutes.
9. Meanwhile in a food processor, add the beans and mushrooms and pulse till smooth.
10. Transfer the beans mixture into a small dish.
11. In a skillet, heat 1 tbsp of the olive oil on medium heat and sauté the garlic till fragrant.
12. Add the beans and mushroom paste and stir to combine.
13. Remove the tomatoes from the oven and keep aside to cool slightly.
14. In a food processor, add the tomatoes and pulse for about 10 seconds.
15. Slowly, add the tomatoes into the skillet, poultry seasoning and the remaining tsp of

tarragon and cook till heated completely.
16. Cook the tortillas in the oven for about 1 minute.
17. Remove the tortillas from the oven and arrange onto a baking sheet.
18. Spread some sauce over the browned side of each tortilla and top with olive slices, followed by the shredded mozzarella cheese.
19. Cook in the oven for about 3-5 minutes.
20. Remove from the oven and keep aside to cool for a few minutes.
21. Cut into quarters and serve.

LEMONY
Greek Cake

🥣 Prep Time: 15 mins
🕒 Total Time: 1 hr 15 mins

Servings per Recipe: 12
Calories   369 kcal
Fat   18.4 g
Carbohydrates   48.7g
Protein   5.1 g
Cholesterol   < 1 mg
Sodium   < 340 mg

Ingredients

cooking spray
1 C. fat free milk
1 tbsp lemon juice
6 egg whites
2 C. sucanat
1 C. light olive oil
1 C. whole wheat flour

1 C. all-purpose flour
1 tbsp lemon zest
1 tsp baking soda
1 tsp salt
1 tsp vanilla extract

Directions

1. Set your oven to 350 degrees F before doing anything else and grease and dust a 9-inch bundt pan.
2. In a small bowl, mix together the milk and lemon juice.
3. In a bowl, add the egg whites and with an electric mixer, beat till stiff peaks form.
4. Add the sucanat and beat till fluffy.
5. Add olive oil and mix till smooth.
6. In another bowl, mix together the flours, lemon zest, baking soda, salt and vanilla extract.
7. Add the egg white mixture, alternating with milk mixture and mix till a smooth mixture forms.
8. Transfer the mixture into the prepared bundt pan evenly.
9. Cook in the oven for about 1 hour or till a toothpick inserted in the center comes out clean.

Saturday Night French Pie

🥣 Prep Time: 20 mins
🕐 Total Time: 40 mins

Servings per Recipe: 6
Calories   304 kcal
Fat   21.6 g
Carbohydrates   19.6g
Protein   8.9 g
Cholesterol   40 mg
Sodium   637 mg

Ingredients

- 1 C. all-purpose flour
- 1/4 tsp salt
- 1/4 C. butter, softened
- 5 fresh basil leaves, chopped
- 3 tbsp olive oil
- 2 tbsp water
- 1 red onion, chopped
- 1 tomato, chopped
- 8 anchovy fillets, chopped
- 8 pitted green olives, chopped
- 6 fresh mushrooms, chopped
- 4 oz. goat cheese
- salt and pepper to taste

Directions

1. In a bowl, mix together the flour, salt and basil leaves.
2. Add the butter, olive oil and water and mix till a smooth dough forms.
3. Refrigerate, covered for about 20 minutes.
4. set your oven to 350 degrees F and grease an 8-inch pie plate.
5. Place the dough in the prepared pie plate and press into the bottom and up the sides till it is about 1/4-inch thick.
6. Cook in the oven for about 8 minutes.
7. Remove the crust from th
8. Arrange the mushrooms and onion in the bottom of the pie crust and top with the tomatoes, olives and anchovies.
9. Place the goat cheese on top in the form of dots.
10. Cook in the oven for about 10 minutes.

MEDITERRANEAN
Burgers

Prep Time: 20 mins
Total Time: 45 mins

Servings per Recipe: 4
Calories   537 kcal
Fat   32.1 g
Carbohydrates   27.4g
Protein   32.6 g
Cholesterol   156 mg
Sodium   1005 mg

Ingredients

1 lb. ground lamb
1 C. crumbled feta cheese
1 large egg
1/2 C. kalamata olives, pitted and sliced
1/8 tsp ground cumin
ground black pepper to taste

4 whole-wheat hamburger buns, toasted if desired

Directions

1. In a bowl, add the lamb, feta cheese, egg, olives, cumin and black pepper and mix till well combined.
2. Make 4 patties from the mixture.
3. Arrange the patties onto the waxed paper lined baking sheet and refrigerate for about 15 minutes.
4. Set your outdoor grill for medium-high heat and lightly, grease the grill grate.
5. Cook the patties on the grill for about 3 minutes per side.
6. Serve these patties over the toasted buns with the topping of your choice.

Italian Mousse

Prep Time: 20 mins
Total Time: 2 hrs 25 mins

Servings per Recipe: 8
Calories   321 kcal
Fat   23.4 g
Carbohydrates   7.3g
Protein   20.8 g
Cholesterol   34 mg
Sodium   747 mg

Ingredients

- 15 pimento-stuffed green olives
- 1 (.25 oz.) package unflavored Jell-O(R)
- 2 (12.5 oz.) cans water-packed tuna, drained
- 1 C. mayonnaise
- 1/2 C. ketchup
- 1/4 tsp paprika
- 1 pinch white pepper
- 1 tbsp white sugar

Directions

1. Grease a small 3-C. terrine with a flat bottom.
2. Cut each stuffed olive into 3-4 slices crosswise.
3. Carefully, place the sliced olives in the bottom of the prepared terrine, making sure that the pimentos stay in the center of the olives.
4. In a small pan, heat 1/2 C. of the water on low heat.
5. Add the gelatin and cook till dissolves completely, stirring continuously.
6. In a blender, add the tuna, mayonnaise, ketchup, paprika, white pepper and sugar and pulse till smooth.
7. Add the gelatin into the mixture and pulse till a smooth paste forms.
8. Carefully, place the tuna mixture over the olives in the terrine.
9. Refrigerate for at least 2 hours.
10. Carefully, remove the tuna mousse from the mold and serve.

MEDITERRANEAN
Olive Hummus

Prep Time: 10 mins
Total Time: 10 mins

Servings per Recipe: 20
Calories   51 kcal
Fat   3.8 g
Carbohydrates   3.7 g
Protein   0.8 g
Cholesterol   0 mg
Sodium   116 mg

Ingredients

1 clove garlic
1 (15 oz.) can garbanzo beans (chickpeas), drained and rinsed
1 (6 oz.) can black olives, drained and liquid reserved
1/4 C. olive oil

Directions

1. In a food processor, add the garlic and pulse till minced.
2. Add the garbanzo beans and pulse till a smooth paste forms.
3. Slowly, add about 2-3 tbsp of the olives liquid, 1 tbsp at a time and pulse till well combined.
4. While the motor is running slowly, add the olive oil and pulse till smooth.
5. Add the olives to the hummus and pulse till the olives are chopped and combined evenly.

Easy Fried Olives

Prep Time: 25 mins
Total Time: 30 mins

Servings per Recipe: 6
Calories   359 kcal
Fat   27.8 g
Carbohydrates   18.3g
Protein   9.9 g
Cholesterol   83 mg
Sodium   1202 mg

Ingredients

1 (15 oz.) can jumbo pitted black olives, drained
4 oz. soft Gorgonzola cheese
2 eggs, beaten
1/4 C. milk
1 C. Italian-style dry bread crumbs
oil for deep frying

Directions

1. Drain the olives well and pat dry with the paper towels.
2. In a pastry bag, place the Gorgonzola cheese and fill into each olive.
3. In a shallow bowl, add the eggs and milk and beat well.
4. In another shallow bowl, place the bread crumbs.
5. Coat the olives with the egg mixture and shake off the excess, then roll in the bread crumbs evenly.
6. In a large pan, heat about 4-inch of oil to 375 degrees F and fry the olives till golden brown.
7. Transfer the olives onto a paper towel lined plate to drain.
8. Keep aside to cool slightly before serving.

MANHATTAN
Party Appetizer

Prep Time: 5 mins
Total Time: 5 mins

Servings per Recipe: 10
Calories 190 kcal
Fat 8.7 g
Carbohydrates 23.1g
Protein 5.3 g
Cholesterol 11 mg
Sodium 507 mg

Ingredients

1 large cucumber
1 (3 oz.) package cream cheese, softened
1/4 C. blue cheese salad dressing
1 (1 lb.) loaf cocktail rye bread

15 pimento-stuffed green olives, chopped

Directions

1. With the tines of a fork, score the unpeeled cucumber lengthwise from all sides.
2. Cut the cucumber into 1/4-inch thick round slices.
3. In a small bowl, mix together the cream cheese and blue cheese dressing.
4. Spread the cheese mixture over the rye bread slices evenly and top with the cucumber and olives evenly.

4-Ingredient Pot Roast Dump Dinner

Prep Time: 15 mins
Total Time: 6 hrs 15 mins

Servings per Recipe: 8
Calories   443 kcal
Fat   25.8 g
Carbohydrates   27.7g
Protein   24.8 g
Cholesterol   81 mg
Sodium   1191 mg

Ingredients

- 2 lb. boneless chuck roast
- 2 (14.5 oz.) cans stewed tomatoes, chopped
- 1 (8 oz.) jar pitted green olives, chopped, 1/3 of liquid reserved
- 8 kaiser rolls

Directions

1. In a slow cooker, place the chuck roast, stewed tomatoes and green olives with the reserved liquid.
2. Set the slow cooker on Low and cook, covered for about 6 hours.
3. Serve the beef mixture over the kaiser rolls.

SOPHIA'S Dream

Prep Time: 1 hr 20 mins
Total Time: 1 hr 30 mins

Servings per Recipe: 36
Calories   68 kcal
Fat   5.1 g
Carbohydrates   3.5g
Protein   2.1 g
Cholesterol   13 mg
Sodium   140 mg

Ingredients

2 C. shredded Cheddar cheese
1/2 C. butter, melted
1 1/4 C. all-purpose flour
36 pimento-stuffed green olives

Directions

1. In a bowl, mix together the Cheddar cheese and flour.
2. Stir in the butter and refrigerate, covered for about 1 hour.
3. Set your oven to 400 degrees F and lightly, grease a baking sheet.
4. Make small balls from the chilled dough.
5. With your thumb, press a deep hole in the center of each ball.
6. Stuff each ball with 1 olive and seal completely.
7. Arrange the balls onto the prepared baking sheet in a single layer.
8. Cook in the oven for about 15-20 minutes, flipping occasionally.

6-Ingredient Olives

Prep Time: 5 mins
Total Time: 1 hr 5 mins

Servings per Recipe: 7
Calories   55 kcal
Fat   5.2 g
Carbohydrates   1.9 g
Protein   < 1.1 g
Cholesterol   2 mg
Sodium   < 245 mg

Ingredients

1 (6 oz.) can black olives, drained
1 clove garlic, minced
1/2 tsp dried basil
1/4 tsp ground black pepper
1 tbsp olive oil
3 tbsp grated Parmesan cheese

Directions

1. In a bowl, add all the ingredients and mix well.
2. Cover the bowl and refrigerate for at least 1 hour.

GREEN OLIVE
Lemon Chicken Breasts

Prep Time: 10 mins
Total Time: 1 hr 30 mins

Servings per Recipe: 4
Calories   216 kcal
Fat   11.2 g
Carbohydrates   4.7g
Protein   25.5 g
Cholesterol   82 mg
Sodium   569 mg

Ingredients

- 2 tbsp butter
- 2 tbsp minced garlic
- 1 large lemon, juiced
- 1/2 tsp dried tarragon
- 4 boneless, skinless chicken breasts
- 20 pitted green olives

Directions

1. Set your oven to 350 degrees F before doing anything else.
2. In an oven-safe pan, melt the butter on medium heat and stir the garlic, lemon juice and tarragon.
3. Add the chicken breasts and cook for about 3-5 minutes per side.
4. Stir in the olives.
5. Transfer the pan into the oven and cook for about 20 minutes.

Potluck Appetizer

Prep Time: 10 mins
Total Time: 25 mins

Servings per Recipe: 7
Calories   340 kcal
Fat   26.7 g
Carbohydrates   15.8g
Protein   10.3 g
Cholesterol   69 mg
Sodium   507 mg

Ingredients

- 2 C. shredded Cheddar cheese
- 1/2 C. butter, softened
- 1 C. sifted all-purpose flour
- 1 tsp paprika
- 1 (6 oz.) can black olives, drained

Directions

1. Set your oven to 400 degrees F before doing anything else and grease a baking sheet.
2. In a bowl, add the cheese, butter, flour and paprika and with an electric mixer, beat till well combined.
3. Roll a tbsp-size pieces of the dough around 1 olive evenly.
4. Arrange the olive balls onto the prepared baking sheet in a single layer.
5. Cook in the oven for about 15 minutes.

GREEK
Veggie Pizza

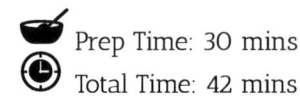

Prep Time: 30 mins
Total Time: 42 mins

Servings per Recipe: 6
Calories   461 kcal
Fat   29 g
Carbohydrates   39.3g
Protein   14.1 g
Cholesterol   36 mg
Sodium   894 mg

Ingredients

- 1/2 C. mayonnaise
- 4 cloves garlic, minced
- 1 C. crumbled feta cheese, divided
- 1 (12 inch) pre-baked Italian pizza crust
- 1/2 C. oil-packed sun-dried tomatoes, coarsely chopped
- 1 tbsp oil from the sun-dried tomatoes
- 1/4 C. pitted kalamata olives, coarsely chopped
- 1 tsp dried oregano
- 2 C. baby spinach leaves
- 1/2 small red onion, halved and thinly sliced

Directions

1. Set your oven to 450 degrees F before doing anything else and arrange an oven rack in the lowest position.
2. In a small bowl, mix together the mayonnaise, garlic and 1/2 C. of the feta.
3. Arrange the pizza crust onto a cookie sheet.
4. Spread the mayonnaise mixture over the pizza crust evenly.
5. Arrange the tomatoes, olives and oregano over the mayonnaise mixture.
6. Cook in the oven for about 10 minutes.
7. In a bowl, add the spinach, onion and the 1 tbsp of the sun-dried tomato oil and toss to coat.
8. Place the spinach mixture over the hot pizza and sprinkle with remaining 1/2 C. of the feta cheese.
9. Cook in the oven for about 2 minutes more.
10. Remove from the oven and cut into 6 equal sized wedges.
11. Serve hot.

Vegetarian Orzo Pesto

Prep Time: 10 mins
Total Time: 25 mins

Servings per Recipe: 2
Calories	828 kcal
Fat	51.1 g
Carbohydrates	65.2g
Protein	30.4 g
Cholesterol	38 mg
Sodium	1618 mg

Ingredients

- 2/3 C. orzo pasta
- 1/2 C. chopped sun-dried tomatoes
- 1/2 C. pitted kalamata olives
- 1/2 C. pesto
- 1/2 C. grated Parmesan cheese
- 1 tbsp olive oil

Directions

1. In a large pan of lightly salted boiling water, cook the orzo pasta for about 11 minutes, stirring occasionally.
2. Drain well and keep aside.
3. In a large bowl, mix together the orzo pasta, tomatoes and olives.
4. Add the pesto and gently, stir to coat.
5. Add the Parmesan cheese and olive oil and gently, stir to coat.

INDIAN
All-Ingredient Crepes

Prep Time: 30 mins
Total Time: 45 mins

Servings per Recipe: 7
Calories   430 kcal
Fat   21.2 g
Carbohydrates   32g
Protein   27.1 g
Cholesterol   155 mg
Sodium   1185 mg

Ingredients

CREPES
1 1/2 C. all-purpose flour
2 1/2 C. milk
3 eggs, beaten
2 tbsp vegetable oil
1/2 tsp salt
FILLING
1/4 C. butter
1 1/4 C. diced celery
1 C. diced onion
2 tbsp all-purpose flour
1 tsp salt
3/4 tsp curry powder
1 C. milk
2 cubes chicken bouillon
1/2 C. warm water
3/4 C. sliced black olives
2 1/2 C. cooked, diced chicken breast meat
1/4 C. freshly grated Parmesan cheese

Directions

1. For the crepes in a medium bowl, add the flour, milk, eggs, oil and salt and beat till a smooth and thin mixture forms.
2. Heat a lightly greased medium skillet on medium heat.
3. Place a thin layer of the mixture and tilt the pan to covers the bottom of the skillet and cook till browned from one side only.
4. Repeat with the remaining mixture. Keep the crepes aside.
5. For the filling in a large skillet, melt the butter on medium heat and sauté the celery and onion till just tender. Add the flour, salt and curry powder and stir till well combined.
6. In a small bowl, dissolve the bouillon in water.
7. In the skillet, add the milk and bouillon mixture and stir till well combined.
8. Stir in the olives and chicken and remove from the heat.
9. Set your oven to 400 degrees F and lightly grease a 13x9-inch baking dish.

10. Place some of the filling mixture onto the center of each crepe, leaving some place from the edges. Fold up the crepes into burrito-style.
11. Arrange the crepe rolls onto the prepared baking dish and sprinkle with the cheese.
12. Cook in the oven for about 12 minutes.

HOW TO MAKE
Deviled Eggs

Prep Time: 20 mins
Total Time: 50 mins

Servings per Recipe: 12
Calories	68 kcal
Fat	5.7 g
Carbohydrates	1g
Protein	< 3.2 g
Cholesterol	94 mg
Sodium	117 mg

Ingredients

6 eggs
3 tbsp mayonnaise
6 pitted Kalamata olives, finely chopped
1 tbsp Dijon mustard
1 tsp lemon juice
1/2 tsp Madras curry powder
1/2 tsp onion powder
1/2 tsp red wine vinegar
1 garlic clove, crushed

Directions

1. In a pan, add the eggs and enough water to cover and bring to a boil.
2. Remove from the heat and keep aside, covered for about 15 minutes.
3. Remove the eggs from the hot water and rinse under cold running water to stop the cooking.
4. Peel the eggs and cut each in half lengthwise.
5. In a bowl, place the egg yolks and with a fork, mash completely.
6. Add the mayonnaise, olives, mustard, lemon juice, curry powder, onion powder, vinegar and garlic and stir to combine.
7. Arrange the egg whites onto a serving platter, cut-side up.
8. Place the yolk mixture into the egg white halves evenly and serve.

Sun Dried Mediterranean Ziti

Prep Time: 15 mins
Total Time: 1 hr

Servings per Recipe: 6
Calories   358 kcal
Fat   7.9 g
Carbohydrates   59.7g
Protein   11.1 g
Cholesterol   1 mg
Sodium   < 180 mg

Ingredients

- 1 (16 oz.) package ziti pasta
- 1/3 C. chopped sun-dried tomatoes
- 1/3 C. black Greek olives, pitted and sliced
- 1/4 C. chopped parsley
- 2 tbsp olive oil
- 2 anchovy fillets, diced
- 2 tsp minced garlic

Directions

1. In a large pan of lightly salted boiling water, cook the pasta till al dente.
2. Drain well and keep aside.
3. Meanwhile in a large serving bowl, mix together the sun-dried tomatoes, olives, parsley, olive oil, anchovy fillets and garlic.
4. Add the pasta and toss to coat.
5. Serve immediately..

KALAMATA
Fettuccini

Prep Time: 30 mins
Total Time: 1 hr

Servings per Recipe: 4
Calories	669 kcal
Fat	28.7 g
Carbohydrates	61.8g
Protein	42.8 g
Cholesterol	69 mg
Sodium	989 mg

Ingredients

8 oz. dry fettuccini noodles
3 tbsp olive oil
1/2 C. finely chopped onion
1/2 C. finely chopped green bell pepper
2 tbsp dried Italian seasoning
1/2 C. pitted kalamata olives
1 lemon, juiced
1 (14.75 oz.) can red salmon, drained
1 (8 oz.) container light sour cream
1 (8 oz.) container low-fat plain yogurt
2 oz. blue cheese, crumbled

Directions

1. In a large pan of lightly salted boiling water, cook the pasta for about 8-10 minutes.
2. Drain well and keep aside.
3. In a large skillet, heat the oil on medium heat and sauté the onion and bell pepper till soft and translucent.
4. Stir in the Italian seasoning, kalamata olives, lemon juice and cook for about 10 minutes.
5. Stir in the salmon, sour cream, yogurt and blue cheese and remove from the heat.
6. Add the cooked pasta and toss to coat well.

A Moroccan Dinner

🥣 Prep Time: 15 mins
🕐 Total Time: 1 hr

Servings per Recipe: 6
Calories   229 kcal
Fat   5.4 g
Carbohydrates   31.2g
Protein   14.1 g
Cholesterol   20 mg
Sodium   1220 mg

Ingredients

1 tbsp olive oil
2 skinless, boneless chicken breast halves - cut into chunks
1/2 onion, chopped
3 cloves garlic, minced
1 (15.5 oz.) can garbanzo beans, drained and rinsed
1 (14.5 oz.) can diced tomatoes with juice
1 (14 oz.) can vegetable broth
1 (14 oz.) can quartered artichoke hearts, drained
1 carrot, peeled and chopped
1/2 C. sliced Mediterranean black olives
1 tbsp white sugar
1 tbsp lemon juice
1 tsp salt
1 tsp ground coriander
1 pinch cayenne pepper

Directions

1. In a large skillet, heat the olive oil on medium heat and cook the chicken, onion and garlic for about 15 minutes.
2. Stir in the garbanzo beans, diced tomatoes with juice, vegetable broth, artichoke hearts, carrot, olives, sugar, lemon juice, salt, coriander and cayenne pepper and bring to a boil.
3. Reduce the heat to low and simmer for about 30 minutes.

FRENCH ITALIAN
Tilapia

Prep Time: 10 mins
Total Time: 25 mins

Servings per Recipe: 4
Calories 453
Fat 216 kcal
Carbohydrates 6.9 g
Protein 1.7g
Cholesterol < 34.8 g
Sodium 62 mg

Ingredients

4 (6 oz.) tilapia fillets
1 tbsp olive oil
1/2 C. chopped tomatoes
5 pitted Kalamata olives, chopped
1 tbsp chopped onion

1 tbsp capers
salt and ground black pepper to taste

Directions

1. Set your oven to 375 degrees F before doing anything else.
2. Coat the tilapia fillets with olive oil and arrange onto a baking sheet.
3. Cook in the oven for about 10-15 minutes.
4. In a small pan, mix together the chopped tomatoes, olives, onion and capers on medium-high heat and cook for about 5-10 minutes, stirring occasionally.
5. Place the tapenade over the baked tilapia fillets and serve.

ENJOY THE RECIPES?

KEEP ON COOKING WITH 6 MORE FREE COOKBOOKS!

Visit our website and simply enter your email address to join the club and receive your 6 cookbooks.

http://booksumo.com/magnet

https://www.instagram.com/booksumopress/

https://www.facebook.com/booksumo/

Printed in Great Britain
by Amazon